Conquering Foreign Languages

An Uncommon Guide to Reaching Fluency in Any Language

By Tristan King

 BIG ACTION BOOKS

BigActionBooks.com

Contents

Introduction

Before we get started: A letter from the author (that's me, Tristan)

Dear fellow language learner,

Great – you've made it to the guide! Thanks for picking it up, and I'm really excited to be able to help you develop your fluency in another language.

I first started learning languages when I was twelve, and I had no idea where it would take me. After more than fifteen years, thousands of hours of study and much laughter at my expense, I've learnt a lot about foreign languages. These days I speak every day with my wife in Spanish, often with friends and colleagues in Japan, and regularly with German friends. I'm learning French at the moment, so I am going through the same process as you (the fourth time around!).

Languages are a huge part of my life, and have given me huge rewards. This isn't to say I have all the answers – far from it - and I still make quirky mistakes all the time. That's all part of the fun.

What I hope to do with this guide is simple: give you practical, useful and fun techniques that will rapidly increase your language skills. They're all relevant regardless of what language you're learning: from Russian to Estonian to Portuguese, almost all of the techniques can be applied across the board. They're not from a textbook, they're not from a university, and they're not from an academic fuddy-duddy who doesn't speak any other languages (you'd be surprised how much linguistic advice comes from people who only speak English, but that's another story).

I used these techniques as I was progressing my languages from beginner to conversational fluency. In particular, I developed many of them while I was learning Spanish, and transformed from a complete newbie to teaching adults within a year, without leaving Australia. All of the techniques are applicable to the real world, and don't take a lot of time or effort.

There's a section at the back of this book with ruled lines, if you'd like to make any notes whilst you're reading the guide.

The goal: make language learning part of your everyday lifestyle.

This is easier than it sounds, and it's my hope that, very soon, you'll be feeling so much more confident with your foreign language. Let's get started.

Tristan King

Who This Guide is For, and Where it Can Take You

Who this guide is for

This guide is intended for anyone interested in learning a foreign language. Specifically, it will help you if you:

- Have tried to learn languages and given up because it was too hard, you didn't have the time, or couldn't find the motivation. I will give you tangible solutions for all of these.
- Are interested, but haven't tried to learn yet because you think it will be too difficult.
- Are learning a language now, but aren't progressing as fast as you want to.
- Have always wanted to visit exotic places and blend in with the locals, or impress your partner who speaks another language.

Where it can take you

The techniques in this guide will help you become fluent faster, feel more confident, and give you ways to practise every day without having to squeeze 'extra' time out of your schedule. These tricks allowed me to develop my Spanish and Japanese to a level where I could work professionally and lead a daily life in those languages.

Most importantly, I'm a believer that anyone can do it.

Don't believe me yet? That's okay. All you need is an open mind. The key is not having innate language learning abilities, slaving over charts for mind-numbing hours or quitting your job to attend weeks of intensive language classes. It's about subtly making the language an ongoing, significant and utterly important part of your everyday lifestyle. Anyone can become fluent by using the right recipe. The goal is to make you sound like a natural.

What This Guide Will Not Do

Although I will recommend other resources along the way, this guide will not deal with:
- How to learn grammar for one particular language. There are plenty of other guides which will help you do that;
- Purely 'traditional' learning techniques, like sitting in a classroom for one hour a week in the hope that fluency will come soon;
- Passive listening. If you don't need to speak or write in your target language, this guide won't help you a lot. It focuses on increasing active language skills.

But wait, who am I to tell you all this? (In case we haven't met yet)
I was born in Australia to English-speaking parents, and I grew up speaking only English. In early high school, Japanese was part of my high school's curriculum, and so began my adventure and passion by coincidence. I continued Japanese through to university, where I was inspired by many great lecturers, students and friends. Since then, I've spent most of my adulthood focusing on languages.

Largely because of the great people who taught and encouraged me, partly due to my stubbornness in achieving my goals, and equally because of the techniques you'll learn in this guide, I've fumbled my way through enough languages to be able to speak with 631 million more people than I could before I started [1].

I speak conversationally fluent Japanese and Spanish, advanced level German, intermediate French, intermediate Italian, and a few snippets of other languages.

Some favourite moments in my language-learning career:
- Seeing the faces of Japanese children when a 187 cm gaigokujin (foreigner) – me - asks them in Japanese how their lunch is going;
- A Japanese colleague who, for a couple of minutes, thought I was a native speaker and asked repeatedly to "put the real Tristan on the phone". This was short-lived, but still put a smile on my face;
- Interacting in Spanish with Colombian friends on my first ever trip to South America, and seeing the smile on their faces when I could manage on my own without a translator;
- Being asked by a drunken German whether I was Swiss (strange, I'll admit - more on this later); and
- Teaching my first Spanish class without having visited a Spanish-speaking country.

Textbook not required

The advice I give isn't coming from a 'textbook' or academic standpoint. My suggestions are all practical and applicable to daily life, and will help you gain fluency faster. I promise I won't lecture you about how important it is to learn grammar, how crucial it is to remember every apostrophe when you write an essay, or how rolling your r's will make-or-break your quest to language domination.

Whilst these are all important, there are plenty of other books which can lecture you about this, and I believe that focusing on them too much is actually detrimental to your language learning. Although I do hold a Masters in Applied Linguistics and a few other official-sounding qualifications [2] I studied many of these after I'd attained fluency in Japanese and Spanish, and reached a reasonably high level of German, so the academic studies are mostly for my own interest and are not necessary to become fluent in a foreign language.

Why I wrote this guide

After many years of in-class and self-induced learning, countless fumbles and plenty of fun, I started noticing friends and colleagues who tried to learn languages and, demoralised, gave up. I found this both puzzling and depressing, so I decided: I wanted to start sharing the techniques that had worked well for me – maybe they could help other people too.

Languages have enriched my life so much that I felt it would be a shame not to share what I've found out. I really want to help people like you achieve their goals in whichever language they are learning. It is my hope that you will learn the techniques, try out what works for you, and soon be embracing the multilingual daily lifestyle.

Of course, everyone learns in different ways, so I'd encourage you to try out the ideas in this guide and apply what works best for you. If you have other techniques that work well, I'd love to hear about them.

A Fire Inside: My Inspiration For Rapid Learning

The beginnings

"Nanniiiiiiiiiiiiiii?!" rang out across the classroom for the third time. We were all still dumbfounded by the bopping introduction music, not so focused on the Japanese conversation booming from the tape recorder. Safe to say, our crew of twelve in Japanese high school class weren't the most attentive language learners (myself included). We'd convinced ourselves that the subject was worth pursuing to get bonus points towards our university entry scores, rather than because we loved grammar and Japanese kanji. High school came to a close. So far so good, but I didn't consider myself very good at learning languages at this point.

In choosing my university course, the possibility of being able to study a language in conjunction with my degree was critical. Having registered, I was surprised to be told by the staff on open day that my course didn't allow elective subjects in the first year. Strange, and it would rule out Japanese. It wasn't until an interview for a completely non-related position that the Head of School told me: "languages are the only exception to this rule". And so it was that my life changed in an instant, now opening up languages as an elective.

I thought it was a 'smart' move to study a language.. Little did I know it would soon become my life's passion. Something changed in me. In high school, I sat in class like a good boy, did my homework and achieved reasonable grades in Japanese, but I wasn't a linguist by any means. Upon taking classes at university with native teachers, movies, music, and lectures in Japanese, I began to feel a fire every time I attended a class. My friends and family thought I was nuts - What was there to get so excited about? - but I started coming out of every class with a silly grin on my face.

And so began my fire.

An accidental introduction
"Sorry, I can't go for lunch." Michael said. "I have to go and attend a seminar about an exchange program."

"Why?" I retorted.

"Well, I thought it might be interesting. Why don't you come?"

And so I went. You can live with a host family, they said. You can enter the cultural program, they said. You can visit castles, make friends, and sing karaoke like a lunatic at three in the morning. Before I knew it, I was writing letters to every local politician and school, trying to get a scholarship to attend the exchange program in Japan. Many polite but unsuccessful replies later, I decided to fund it myself, and came back after three months with a few extra kilos and a high level of Japanese, which I continued to work on at University.

What does all this have to do with rapid learning? I knew that I loved studying Japanese, but I didn't know why. A trip to Germany then enticed me to study some German. Turns out, I loved that too.

When I met a Colombian girl a couple of years later through a mutual friend, and we started seeing each other, I thought I should try my hand at Spanish. After all, I'd had a little practice at learning languages - why not try another? My newfound Colombiana's male friends had already taught me all there was to know about terrifyingly rude Spanish, and insisted on making this innocent-sounding Spanish-speaker-wannabe showcase his newfound language abilities, much to the amusement of all who understood. Ruder words had never been spoken at the Hard Rock Cafe dinner table.
Several polite requests from my girlfriend later, I started to realise that I had better start on some Spanish which wasn't going to land me in a fight or in accidental trouble with the in-laws. After she moved back to Colombia for four months with our relationship intact and plans to return to Melbourne, I decided to spend those months getting my Spanish up to scratch, in an effort to better understand her and be able to communicate with her family and friends. Two years later, I said my wedding vows to her in Spanish.

It was during this period that I started to realise how I could accelerate my language learning, picking up vocabulary, the humour of the language, grammar and cultural subtleties in a way much faster than I had before. Japanese had taken me ten years to learn to a conversational level. Spanish, less than one. This guide will show you how.

For Your Reading Pleasure
These techniques can be applied to any language (not just one, or two)

This guide is not focused on any one language. It's not geared to teach you vocabulary or grammar from one language in particular. Why? Because the techniques are applicable to any language.

I will reference Japanese, German and Spanish often, because they are the languages I speak: but the techniques will always be phrased in such a way that they can be applied to any language, and I encourage you to use my examples as exactly that: examples. All instances I use in this guide could easily be replaced with samples from Russian, Indonesian or Latvian, and the techniques would be equally as applicable.

A Cautionary Note: The Internet Alone Won't Get You Booking Hotels in Portuguese
As you will see, I am a big advocate of using the internet and other tools to improve fluency, so much so that they inspired me in part to write this guide. However, I must begin with a word of caution: some websites will have you believe that the internet alone will allow you to speak with locals very soon after taking their online courses. Whilst I am a firm believer in the benefits of online resources, this approach needs to be taken with caution. I do not believe it is possible to become fluent using the Internet alone.

Enough disclaimers. Let's move on to the mischief.

PART I. The Beauty Of Beginning

NAGANO, JAPAN, 2006

"Kazuma, iru?" Oi, is Kazuma there, or what?
I cringed, and wondered how this must have sounded to the Japanese receptionist. I was working in a Japanese hotel, and my Australian friend was innocently asking whether the owner's son was available. I imagined the listener giving a slight cringe and thinking about how to respond. My friend was inquiring about the whereabouts of the second-highest ranked person in the entire organisation, the owner's son, using the most casual Japanese in the universe.

My friend spoke very well, and was always well-liked by everyone. She'd learned her Japanese from friends and colleagues over a period of a few years, so she wasn't aware (nor interested in) the honorifics and other forms of Japanese that allow one to show respect and be polite. Had she asked "Kazuma-san irasshaimasuka", "Is Mr. Kazuma there, please?", her Japanese would have been elevated to another level.

It's still admirable, and lots of people acquire language in this way. I'm not discouraging it. But if we want to be mistaken for locals, feel comfortable and fit in when speaking another language, we have to start with the basics: some good old-fashioned human interaction.

Starting Out: Good Old-Fashioned Human Interaction
As much as many who despised blackboards and chalk in school will shudder to think about, the best way to get started is to take some basic classes. "That's not very practical advice from a guide about rapid language learning" I hear you thinking. You're right. It's an obvious but integral part of your learning process.

Why? Without basic grammar and workings of the language, it is extremely difficult to reach real fluency. I have several friends who get their meaning across very well in different languages, but because they didn't learn the grammar and structure in the beginning, they fell into the admirable habit of 'make it up as you go along' and are now loveable dead-giveaways for a non-native speaker. This in itself is also an outstanding accomplishment - but our goal here is to make you sound like a natural.

So the first step is to find a reputable language school and study for a few weeks to get your artistic brain ready for rapid fire mode.

Choosing a Language School

Most major cities have reputable, well-known schools for the most popular languages. I have personally had excellent experience with all of these. Goethe Institut and Alliance Française are two such schools, both with outstanding curriculums and even better teaching staff. Choose a school which tells you the curriculum up front and has a focus on useful language learning rather than rote methods that ask you to spend countless hours mindlessly memorising facts or words. It's also worthwhile searching online for reviews of the school prior to enrolling – see what others have said.

When choosing a school, try to find one that has a clear segmentation of levels and milestones after each: After Level One, you will be able to introduce yourself, speak in the present tense, and talk about your hobbies; After Level Two, you will be able to speak in the past, talk about your family, and order your favourite brand of coffee. And so on. It doesn't matter exactly what the milestones are, as long as they are known and achievable.

If your chosen language is not covered by a well-known school, not to worry. Private tutors are often a great option, where low-cost professionals will meet at a mutually convenient time and place. Choose one who demonstrates experience, has a good working knowledge of the learning process, and who will let you customise your curriculum. Tutors all over the world are now advertising on popular web directories and employment websites tutor sites. A quick trip to local universities, schools or notice boards in your area can often yield quick leads to tutors too.

Intensive or Non-Intensive?

Personally, I find intensive classes to be the fastest way to kick start learning. Four quick-hitting weekends of three to four hours later, you've completed what would normally take three months. It's satisfying, and often allows you to group your knowledge together because you haven't forgotten what you studied at the beginning of the term. If intensive courses aren't your cup of tea or you don't have the time, the techniques coming up will guide you through how to learn quickly in standard classes.

What I want you to remember

Classes are an important part of kick starting language learning. Taking them simultaneously - whether it be one, two, or seven hours per week - while you employ the techniques in the following chapters, will get you the best results. Classes go hand in hand with lifestyle integration of languages.

Learning Verb Tables: Do I Haveeee To?

In many languages, one step to fluency is learning how to conjugate verbs. I don't know many people who enjoy conjugating verbs [3], or any other necessary part of rote-learning a language. Fortunately, there are ways to speed up this necessary evil. Here's my method of tackling verbs and vocabulary:

Take out one page of A4 paper. Draw a small table with a few columns. Write the verb up the top, and the subjects (I, you, he, she, we, they) down the left hand side.

Fill in the conjugations one-by-one, and take note of the endings. The verb itself (underlined in the picture below) is what we're practising. Here's an example, with the French verb "aller", "to go":

French: "aller", to go.

Je vais (I go)
Tu vas (You go)
il, elle va (he/she goes)
nous allons (we go)
vous allez (you pl. go)
ils, elles vont (they go)

Then do it again. And again. Are you bored yet? If so, that's good: the sooner you learn it, the sooner you can start using it! If you're getting bored of conjugating it, chances are it's sinking in. If you conjugate the verb six times on paper (writing it out, the same as the picture above), and use it in a sentence six times in real conversation, you will remember it. You can do the paper conjugation in five minutes, and vary the speaking part over a few days or in one of your language classes. Take it one verb at a time, and soon they'll start flowing. Give it a try.

Light a Fire: Finding Your Inspiration

To really become fluent in any language, it helps to find a passion point. For me, this was finding my wife and listening to music (Spanish), Japanese cuisine and culture (Japanese) and, I'm not ashamed to admit, the wonderful creamy wheat-beer served with healthy doses of Oompah music in Germany (German). Lately, the simply wonderful sound of French accents has me hooked on learning French, and the idea of one day sounding like French-speakers do. Spend a few minutes thinking about where your passion really lies. This will not change you in an instant, but it's amazing how quickly, given the right material, you can build up your language abilities. Here are some suggestions:

Friends and Lovers (or both)
Do you have any friends, family who speak your target language? How about someone you're trying to get closer to? Imagine yourself being able to have a fluent conversation with them. Friends are usually extremely encouraging, and will laugh along the way as you learn by making mistakes. Added benefits of speaking with friends include being able to have a private conversation anywhere (you and your friend conversing in fluent Russian on a train packed with non-Russian speakers) and visiting them in their home country. Had I not been able to speak Spanish during my first trip to meet my Colombian in-laws, I would have been sitting like a little boy in the corner for four weeks. Being able to actively converse with everyone made my trip all the more worthwhile, and established my in-laws as close friends for life.

Get Arthouse
Do you like art? For those of us so inclined, different cultures can open a world of possibilities. Consider looking into writers, painters, poets and other artists who've produced work in your target language. Movies are also a fantastic way to practise (you can start with the subtitles on, and turn them off as you become more confident and/or daring). Most language schools have libraries where DVDs, guides and magazines can be borrowed for free; several of the larger schools also hold regular art exhibitions and showcase works from speakers of the target language.

Shake Your Tail Feather

If there is one defining, pain free and unconscious vocab-booster, it is music. Listening to music in Spanish exponentially increased my vocabulary with little conscious effort. Listening to the language with a melody transforms the words from simple vocab into meaningful pieces of language. There are some words now that I can't even say without singing the melody. (This makes me sound quite silly in conversations sometimes.) Explore international bookshops for non-English CDs, listen online, or visit iTunes to download artists onto your iPod or other MP3 player. (More on this later.)

Jump in the deep end: Travel

Best of all: travel to a destination which speaks your chosen language. Doesn't this seem terribly obvious? I agree. But I have the feeling that many people consider this an impassable obstacle due to time or costs. The fact is, thousands of universities and language schools have cooperative programs with sister cities, offering low-cost language programs. Large language schools also offer international exchange options.

In 2008, I requested a month of annual leave to attend an exchange program in Bonn, Germany. What I thought would be an endless tirade of negotiation turned out to be easier than I thought - my boss even gave me one week's extra paid 'personal leave' to encourage me to pursue my passion.

Consider the possibility of exploring the art and music you've become inspired by, making new friends and jumping into the deep end by speaking with natives who don't speak English. This sounds daunting, but is the single most effective way of getting fluent fast.

If travel isn't your cup of tea or possible for you right now, don't fret. This guide is about becoming fluent without having to leave your home country.

Embracing the Quirkiness of Languages

Headbreakers, illicit enrichment, and electronic conversations
SPANISH CLASS, MELBOURNE, 2009

"It's called WHAT?!"

Three of my eight students were looking at me with puzzled looks on their faces.

"A headbreaker. Don't you love it?" I stated again, my happiness at this fact growing ever more obvious.

"Because it can break your head if you don't understand it. Get it?!"

Gradually, they relented, accepted that I wasn't making it up, and smiled all at the same time. "This is why I love teaching Spanish", I thought to myself. "And why I leave every class with a grin on my face, even if it's at 10pm".

My students had learned a new word - 'rompecabezas', the 'headbreaker', meaning "Puzzle" in Spanish. A headbreaker, because it can break your head, you see? ;-)

Before you write me off as a raving, repetitive madman, allow me to get to the point: embracing the quirkiness of languages not only makes them all the more loveable and fun, it helps you to learn faster.

My students only needed to hear this word a couple of times to have it burned into their memory. It was so strangely funny and wonderful at the same time that I remembered it instantly too.

Words which don't have the same structure or meaning in direct translation can sometimes throw us off, or discourage us because they're so different. Rather than seeing this as a setback, I suggest giving in to the fact that all languages are different, and embracing it 100% for your own amusement and speed of learning. The more you can differentiate between your target language and native language, the faster you will move from word-for-word translation to fluently speaking your new language.

Embracing fun and quirky examples is a fantastic part of the language learning process, and you can use it to your advantage by laughing about strange terms, and finding ways to remember them. Here are some of my other favourite examples, with the literal translation in italics and real meaning in brackets:

- Enriquisimiento illicito: illicit enrichment of oneself (Fraud/embezzlement in Spanish)
- Denwa: electronic conversation (Telephone in Japanese)
- Geflügelpfanne: winged animal dish (German, a meat-lover's assortment of chicken, duck, potatoes and sauerkraut found in select German beer halls)

Action Plan

1. If you haven't already, investigate language courses in your local area. Consider intensive versus non-intensive, and private tutoring if schooling isn't available or convenient.

2. Think about two concrete ways you can increase the connection and passion with your target language. Music, Art, Movies, or something else, I'm sure you can do it.

3. Find and use three quirky words or phrases from your target language over the next week. Try to find phrases which contain one or two words you already know.

4. Purposely surprise a speaker of your target language with your new quirky phrase, and watch their face light up.

5. If you're learning verbs, practise them repeatedly for ten minutes using the technique mentioned earlier. Write them in a table with the verb on the left, and fill the table in a few times. No pain, no gain. Just think: in the time it takes you to watch a 30 minute reality TV show, you can probably memorise 8 verbs, forever.

PART II. Mind-Bending: How to Skyrocket Your Language Skills (And Other Interrogations)

GERMAN CLASS, SYDNEY, 2007

I stared at the list of words in dismay. Next week's test was going to include recall of the words "Naturopathy", "Mercury Poisoning", "Essential Oils" and "Botanical Medicine".

Hmm. There's a lesson to be learnt here, I thought. My head was already hurting from last week's vocabulary list. Once I realised it was far more effective to filter for what I needed than to try and remember everything "just in case", I began to feel better. I wasn't planning on getting mercury poisoning from essential oils and fixing it with naturopathy and a healthy dose of botanical medicine any time soon, so I dropped those and focused on the vocab I was more likely to use.

(No hard feelings to any naturopaths: I'm just not planning to be one myself.)

This brings us to some techniques to help you memorise what matters.

Super-Boosting Vocabulary (and how Robert De Niro helped my Spanish)

Once you've taken some basic classes, the next big challenge for many learners is remembering new words and phrases. I've found two specific techniques that help me remember words very quickly and retain them:

1. Only try to remember vocabulary you think you will actually use.
How often will you discuss cures for world hunger in your newfound tongue? What about buying bread? Choose the bread. There's little point slaving over long lists of vocabulary if you think you'll rarely use those words. As your mental word list exponentially builds up, you'll have the chance to add more and more words as you gain confidence. In the beginning, only focus on words you think you'll use in the near future - with friends, classmates, teachers, penpals or newfound lovers. Whoever it is, focus on what you will actually use, and ignore the rest for now.

2. Make word associations with 'like-sounding' words.
Psycholinguistics (the study of how language works within the human brain) has proved that linking words by their sound ("phonetic association" for language geeks like me) is much more effective than memorising by meaning ("semantic association"). When you hear a new word, try to link it to the sound of a word you know in your native language, which has a meaning that will help you retain the word. No matter how silly, strange or quirky they may be, use it anyway. In fact, the more laughable they are, the more effective.

Some examples:
- The word for 'money' in Spanish: 'dinero'. Who do I know of that has a lot of money? Robert De Niro sure does. And his name sounds awfully like the word dinero. Ka-ching, One word remembered.

   Money = Robert Dinero = Dinero in Spanish.

- The word for 'violent' in Japanese: 'rambō', らんぼう. Who reminds me of being violent? This guy:

   Yep, Rambo [4] was definitely violent, and his name is almost exactly the same as the Japanese word, but with an elongated 'o' sound on the end.

   Violent = Rambo = **Rambō** in Japanese

I told you they were silly. But over the years, thousands of such word associations have entered my brain. After a while, these associations simply disappear and the word becomes natural. In the beginning, it's extremely important to find something you can relate to. If you have to invent fun ways to do this, so be it.

Seek and you shall find: Interrogating your way to the top

MONASH UNIVERSITY, MELBOURNE, 2003

She was looking at me as though I had just asked the silliest question on earth.

"Yes, but what's the translation?", I foolishly asked, again.

"Don't ask me that. Ask me how I would rephrase it in Japanese. Translating directly won't help you."

Yamada sensei [5] had a reputation for being one of the toughest lecturers in Monash University's advanced Japanese program. She (quite rightly) picked on people who hadn't done their homework, and was very strict in speaking to us in Japanese.

Unbeknownst to me at the time, I was trying to defeat myself, and she had caught me out.

How to dramatically increase your practice time and get the information you want, fast

I had been fishing for a translation from a difficult Japanese phrase into English. Seems like a reasonable request to a native Japanese-speaking senior lecturer, right? Wrong! In the first class of almost every language course, we're taught how to ask "What does XYZ mean?" right off the bat. Most of us – myself included in the beginning – make the mistake of thinking "my [teacher/lecturer/friend/whoever] knows how to speak English. It's much easier to get the translation, and I'll remember it better that way".

In fact, this is an excellent way of *reducing* the amount of vocabulary you can remember.

If you already have five, a hundred, five thousand, or however many words at your disposal, why not use them? This point alone will bring you enormous benefits in memory retention, not to mention speaking practice.

This brings us to our rule of interrogation: ask for things to be rephrased in your target language. Don't focus on the English translation.

If you're starting out, get used to asking "How do I say XYZ" in the target language.

BAD: "How do I say [featherweight champion] in Spanish?"

GOOD: "Como se dice [featherweight champion] en español?"

Here, you have practised five Spanish words ('como', 'se', 'dice', 'en' 'español' = five words), compared to zero in the "BAD" example.

Once you start using this much-neglected technique, your vocabulary will skyrocket and people will naturally speak to you more in your target language.

But what if I don't understand the answer?

This is a fear all language learners have. I know I do. Here's a common scenario:
1. Jen walks into gelato shop in Milan
2. Jen, trying to be proactive, asks in perfect Italian "How much is a gelato cone?"
3. Nice Italian man, noting Jen's fluent Italian, responds: "Wowyour Italianisverygood! Thecostdependsonwhich flavouryouwouldike wehavestrawberrylemonand limewhichdoyouwant anddoyouwant adoublecone?"
4. Jen smiles, waves her hand and leaves the gelato shop, overwhelmed by the response and disappointed at not being able to understand the question.

I can't blame her. This situation comes up often when learning a language. The key: use it as a chance to make a friend, practice, and still get what you want. I guarantee you will pick up more words from context, and accidentally come away at least one word better than when you asked your first gelato question.

Let's look at this situation again:

1. Jen walks into gelato shop
2. Jen asks, in perfect Italian "How much is a gelato cone?"
3. Nice Italian man responds the same as before
4. Jen smiles politely, and again in Italian says "Sorry, could you please speak a little more slowly?"
5. Italian man obliges: "Perdon. What flavour would you like? (Pointing at flavours)"
6. Jen reads "Strawberry" from the red ice cream tub, and says "fragola"
7. Italian man says "Sure!" and proceeds to get delicious ice cream.

The result: Jen has a delicious ice cream in-hand, learnt the word for "Strawberry" and will remember it because it tasted good. The Italian man got a new customer and a smile from a nice girl who made an effort to speak his language.

To some people, this comes naturally. I'm envious of them. For the rest of us, it's a conscious effort to keep our eye on the prize: practice. I find this to be a major stumbling block among my students and language-learning friends. Try it out, and use the beginner's phrases we often forget after the first class – "excuse me", "how do you say [X]", "please speak more slowly", and "what does that mean?". You might even get some delicious ice cream.

Searching For Opposites: A Fool-Proof Way to Elicit Words from Friends & Strangers

Omnipresent opposites

One of the most useful techniques for smooth conversation is finding opposites. Often, you'll know a word in your target language (e.g. "logical"), but not its opposite ("illogical"). Let's look at two scenarios.

Imagine this conversation is happening in your target language:

SCENARIO #1: We don't ask for the opposite

A: "I was trying to explain to my father why his argument wasn't logical. I want a pet monkey, and that's that."

B: "And he wasn't getting it?"

A: "No, he was being so.... mmmmm.... what do you call it when someone isn't giving a normal argument that makes any sense? I can't remember the word for it..."

The last sentence, with umming and lengthy questions doesn't sound very natural and completely breaks the conversation away from getting our monkey.

SCENARIO #2: Ask for the opposite

A: "I was trying to explain to my father why his argument wasn't logical. I want a pet monkey, and that's that."

B: "And he wasn't getting it?"

A: "No, he was being so… what's the opposite of logical?"

B: "Illogical"

A: "Yes, that. Illogical. He was being so illogical. I was trying to tell him that…"

In the second example, asking for the opposite keeps the conversation flowing. It's quick, sharp, and we now have a new word in our vocabulary, which we can use next time.

Using Downtime to Skyrocket Your Fluency

MELBOURNE, AUSTRALIA, 2010

"Want to hear what I learnt today?" I asked the same as yesterday, and the day before that, and the day before that. I was on a roll. Would today be a fizzer, or a winner? My wife nodded curiously, in anticipation of the snippet I'd learnt that day.

"Se te va a escapar el pajarito! Tienes la cremallera abierta."

Your little birdie is about to escape you! Your fly is open.

She smiled and looked at me with an expression that said "I know I'm going to be hearing this one again. What irresponsible human being taught that to you, a beginner Spanish learner?".

A clear winner. Pleased, I smiled and committed that one to memory. It was a sure thing when I travelled to Colombia and tried it out on some (open minded) friends, who looked at me a little strangely while still laughing. Don't worry - their flies weren't really open. It was all hypothetical.

That's one phrase I definitely would never have learned from a guide, or in a classroom. I'll admit, not everyone needs or wants to know phrases like this. I'm not advocating that everyone should learn how to talk about zippers. But how I learnt this is much more exciting, and will boost your speaking and listening to a level beyond what you thought possible: podcasts. If you haven't exploited them to improve your language skills yet, in the next section I'll try and convince you to do just that.

A Match Made in Heaven: Podcasts and "Downtime"

I have found that the single most effective tool for getting fluent fast is by finding and listening to little snippets of audio called "podcasts". Readers from the iPhone age may be familiar with this on some level; if you're not, the next two pages will turn you into an expert in under five minutes.

[If you're already listening to a great language podcast, you can say hooray, and safely skip the next couple of pages.]

What podcasts are, and how they will help
A podcast is a piece of recorded audio that can be played on almost any device. Usually, you download them through a computer or new-generation mobile phone, and play them on some sort of portable device. I listen to them on my iPhone, but almost all modern mobile phones and MP3 players will allow you to listen to podcasts.

If you don't have one, you can get yourself an MP3 player for under $30 at most electronic retailers, and even cheaper if you use a website like eBay. There's no need to get into the technical details of the file: all you need to know is, a podcast is an audio file you can listen to on a mobile phone, computer, or MP3 player.

This means you don't have to be staring into a book, talking on the phone with a native speaker, or sitting in a musty classroom to be learning. Beautiful in its simplicity, this opens up a world of possibilities for language learning.

In the last few years, hundreds of companies have dedicated their core business to producing podcasts. They're not few and far between, and it's not little Johnny sitting in his room with a tape recording, speaking into a low-quality microphone. High quality podcasts (the ones we'll be finding) offer structured lessons, with different levels to allow you to build up, interesting subject matter and are, above all, fun.

Get yourself some podcasts in under ten minutes

Think it sounds complicated? I promise, it's not. Here's how to get podcasts and start boosting your language.

Where to get them

The best resource is iTunes. Search "Language Learning" or the name of your target language in the "Podcast" section, and several podcasts will likely appear at the top. If you don't see any there, try Googling "podcast [name of your language]". (I don't like recommending "Google XYZ", as it is usually obvious, but this really is the best way to find them outside of iTunes.)

Different levels

Most good podcasts offer a series of different levels. You can, for example, start off with "newbie" or "beginner" level podcasts, and work your way up to intermediate and advanced levels as you get more comfortable. I wouldn't suggest going straight to the higher levels, as it can be discouraging. Once you're on the verge of understanding everything, move up quickly to keep challenging yourself.

To pay, or not to pay?

The large majority of podcasts I've used are free, and I believe there are plenty of free resources out there that allow you to learn without paying a cent. Most paid podcasting companies offer at least a free trial of one-week or a set number of podcasts. I'd highly recommend checking these out first, before you commit to anything paid. I did pay for a podcasting service while I was learning Spanish (about $12 per month), and it was well worth it because they produced great content and I listened to them every day. Try a couple of podcasts out first, and then consider if the investment is right for you. Many podcasting services also offer all of their files for free, in the hope that you'll purchase some other products from them. This is great because you can get all of their audio completely gratis.

Devices (how to listen)
Most mobile phones will play MP3 files. If yours isn't compatible (i.e. doesn't allow you to plug into a computer and add audio files such as music), and you don't want to shell out for an expensive mp3 player, you can purchase a low-cost MP3 player for less than $30 at most retail outlets, and possibly even cheaper on eBay. Another good option is to simply play them on your computer (I do this while I'm cooking), or borrow a friend's player.

Now it's even easier - thousands of language-related podcasts are available on streaming services like Spotify, Apple Music, Stitcher, and other players like Overcast.

So, When Am I Going To Listen To All This?: Downtime Is Your Friend.
Downtime is any time where you're not really doing anything with your mind other than thinking. Standing on the tram or train, riding your bike around the lake, watering the garden, going for a run, or sitting at your desk and procrastinating are all examples of downtime. For me, using this time productively by listening to podcasts was the single most important tool to bringing my Spanish from beginner to fluent in under a year. I listened to hundreds of podcasts, often up to five per day, until it all sunk in.

I wasn't creating downtime out of thin air either. I was still working a job 8.30-5.30 every day, had an active social life, a girlfriend, and did everything I would normally do in a day. I just used the downtime to my advantage.

Extra stuff that sometimes comes with podcasts
Some companies offer PDF transcripts with podcasts. If you're having trouble picking up the words, or just want some visual affirmation of what's being said, these can be a great resource. I suggest listening to the podcast once through before you look at the written transcript: this trains you to listen intensely at first, and your revision will be more effective.

Integrating the learnings from podcasts with your classes
After you listen to a few podcasts, you'll find that some of the content overlaps with what you're learning in your classes. This is great, because it reaffirms what you've been studying, gives it some real-world context, and allows you to revise. If you can, listen to podcasts that relate to what you're doing in class.
Ok, I'm convinced.. but how do I get podcasts?

Rather than list out all the steps in this guide, I'd suggest:
- Apple Users (iPods, iPhones, etc.):
  http://www.apple.com/itunes/podcasts/fanfaq.html
- Non-Apple Users: It depends on your device, but usually you simply plug the device into your computer, and drag the files you want onto the device. Check out your device's instructions.

It isn't difficult, and takes less than five minutes. [6]

Beating The "Kill Me Now" Classroom Moment

Sixteen pale, blank faces jolt up all at once like a new event at the Olympics: "synchronised panicking". On each desk lies a piece of paper with the first examination question. The look on each of these faces says something like "Kill me now, please. Why do I have to learn grammar like this?".

The dreaded exam question causing the perfectly-timed synchronised panic?
"Form sentences by conjugating these transitive verbs in the past progressive subjunctive'.
I'd be trembling in my boots, too.

This scene is repeated hundreds of times each year in universities, language schools and classrooms the globe over.

A necessary evil

Am I going to tell you not to take these tests? No. Am I going to suggest that you riot in the classroom, set fire to the exam and storm out without answering the question?

Unfortunately not. The fact is, we need to know and learn these (albeit annoying) pieces of grammar if we want to sound natural. Teaching grammar is a necessary evil. The good news is, there are many ways to overcome this panic state, and all you need is one example you can relate to.

Slaying the grammatical dragon

"I can teach Japanese to a monkey in 46 hours. The key is just finding a way to relate to the material." - Rubin Carver, Road Trip (2000)

Although grammar in any language can be overwhelming (and is one of the top reasons why most language learners don't make it past the second or third level), the key is finding a way to relate to it. Try not to get caught up on the denseness of the grammar. Also realise that almost all of the seemingly-complex grammatical structures also exist in English. You use them every day without thinking about it.

I'm not getting on my high horse about grammar here – I still find grammar challenging (especially in German) - but there are ways to climb over the wall so it doesn't cause a roadblock.

Find one example you can relate to, stick to it, and apply it. From there, all the technical-sounding instructions fade away and you'll be able to concentrate without being pale-faced. Here are some specific examples, with the "Panic-instiller" being the grammar structure that tends to make us want to run out of the classroom:

Panic-instiller: "Formulate a sentence in the causative tense"
Causative just means when you "cause" someone to do something else. You make, force, or let them do something.
- The police **made** the bank robber go to jail (sent him to jail);
- My brother **let me** borrow his car;
- We **forced** the monkey to give back our hard-earned biscuits.

Panic-instiller: Subjunctive
When you're talking about something that isn't certain, when there's an element of doubt, or we cannot be 100% sure that something is going to happen. The great Ben Curtis from Notes in Spanish relates this to two people: a hippie (who isn't sure about anything, and is very relaxed), and a classroom teacher who says everything factually and in concrete terms.

- We'll stop wherever we can (not one specific place, who knows where);
- If I were you (I'm not, but if I were…);
- If I had the opportunity to go to Paris, I'll do [X] (who knows if I will, maybe one day, and if so, I'll do [X]).

These are just two examples, and this guide isn't all about grammar, so I'll stop there before the grammarians chime in. These individual grammatical structures require much more in-depth explanation than what's here for a full understanding.

The key point is: when you're learning intimidating grammar, remember:
Learn the structure (e.g. "causative") once -- learn to recognise it -- relate it to something you know -- pick one example, and apply it.

Action Plan

1. Start making associations with like-sounding words, especially for words you find difficult. Think hard. There is usually a word that sounds similar and will help you with the meaning. Remember, the sillier the better (a-la Robert Dinero and Rambo).

2. Use the phrases you were taught in the first class: "How do you say [X]", "Can you speak more slowly?", and so on, in your target language. Don't ask the teacher in English any more.

3. Next time you're stuck on a word, use the "opposites" technique to get the word you want and keep the conversation flowing.

4. Download at least three episodes of a podcast related to your language, and use downtime to listen to them. If you like them, consider downloading more on a regular basis.

5. Before your next test (or challenging piece of homework, if you don't have tests), make sure you have at least one example of each piece of grammar you're being tested on. Don't get flustered – use this single example to draw a link to the grammatical concept.

PART III. To Become Fluent, Speak You Must

The Best Strategy to Conquer Your Target Language

So far, we've talked about several techniques to help skyrocket your vocabulary, break down grammar barriers and get through conversations more smoothly. After you know the bare basics of a new language, the most important technique is to make it, one way or another, a part of your everyday lifestyle. I know, this sounds ominous. It sounds big, and it sounds complicated. Truth be told, anyone can do it, it doesn't take a lot of time, and it doesn't take a lot of effort. All it takes is a shift of mindset: focus on the language, and your fluency will shoot up faster than you had ever imagined. Next we'll look at several fast, low-cost and simple ways you can do this.

If you remember nothing else from this guide, remember this: the fastest way to dominate your language is to make it a part of your everyday lifestyle.

Creative, free methods to make learning part of every day
Here are all the techniques I used in boosting my languages from beginner to intermediate to advanced:

Visit Multicultural Events
Most cities (especially larger cities) have several events each year related to culturally diverse groups. Simply by coming into contact with native speakers, you'll often be invited to such events. They're also usually supported by local language schools, who tend to promote them to their students. Take advantage. Here are some ideas:
- Food festivals. Example: there are two Latin American food festivals in Melbourne run by two separate organisations. I usually attend both to practise my Spanish, see salsa dancers perform moves my body can't cope with, and eat Latin treats.
- Film festivals. Often sponsored by language schools, such as the Alliance Française for French and Goethe Institut for German. Try the web, ask at your local language school, or speak to friends who speak your language, and you're sure to hear about upcoming film festivals.
- Conversation nights. Language Schools often hold these to encourage conversation (and of course, enrolments). Although they sound intimidating, they tend to cater for beginners and be made up of 'games' rather than forcing you to deliver a speech. My experience with these has been 100% positive. Often, they're free and even provide a drink or two.

Speak to strangers

Some people think I'm strange. I do sometimes initiate conversation with strangers if I hear them speaking in Spanish, German or Japanese. Have I ever had anyone ignore me, or think I was rude because of this? Never. Not once. Am I nervous before I do it? Sure.

You'll be surprised how much people will appreciate you making the effort, and the practice that goes on in your head before you initiate conversation is a great way to get your brain ticking over.

Encourage your classmates

It's easy to default to English after you leave class, or when the teacher isn't listening. Try not to do this, and your language skills will improve exponentially. Encourage your classmates to speak to you in your target language, too.

Be a teacher's pet

I've been called a teacher's pet plenty of times. No problem for me. As far as I'm concerned, teachers are there because they want to help you learn, because they're passionate about the language (some, not all), and because they get paid (yes, all). Use them to your advantage. I am one of those annoying people in class who asks detailed questions, requests extra exercises and doesn't shut up until I understand (although sometimes I'll do this before or after class, so I don't get on everyone's nerves).

I may be a teacher's pet, but I think this is one of the main reasons why I have gone on to the higher levels of language classes when other people have retired at the first or second level. Friends who have gone on to advanced levels have also been good at asking lots of questions.

Play Dr. Dolittle

It gets weirder. Speaking to animals? You can't be serious? Yes, I am. I talk to my pets all the time, and even other peoples' pets if they don't throw me out of the house. The point? It's not important that everyone you speak with understands you perfectly. The goal is to speak and think in your target language every day.

We all speak to our pets in some way – if you're going to be saying phrases like "Good boy", "I'm home", "Dinner time", "Get down from there", or "Put that shoe down", why not say them in your target language instead of English? It'll be at least another thirty words you can practise every day. After doing this, I found that the phrases I used with pets became much easier. Unfortunately for my cat, the one I used most was "urusai na~", or "you're such a noisy boy". I think he got the message.

Creative Labelling and Placement

"My roommates didn't know what hit them."

An old roommate of mine wasn't shy in telling me how she perfected her French. Everything in her kitchen was labelled with post-it notes: pots, pans, the oven, the fridge, all with post-it notes in French. She learnt the names of all her kitchen utensils very quickly using this visual reinforcement.

When I was learning Spanish, I put up the irregular verb charts in the shower (posted on the outside of the glass, facing inwards). Now, when I conjugate irregular verbs in Spanish, I remember those verb charts because I spent ten minutes every day for a month looking at them. Irregular, no more.

Why Bill Gates and Steve Jobs Want You to Conquer Languages Too

Have a computer, an iPod or a mobile phone? These can all teach you hundreds of words very quickly. Why? Because, most of the time, you know exactly what all of the menus already say and do. If you're anything of a laptop-dweller like me, you already know the menus in Microsoft Word, the iPhone Interface, and Google Chrome in your sleep.

Even if you don't, you'll be able to guess with 90% accuracy in another language. I've learned hundreds of words across three languages this way, without even trying. Some examples: available (from MSN messenger status), file (almost every menu in every program has this item), insert, edit, view, settings, and so on. Several of these words are useful in an everyday context, which is what makes this technique so powerful.

Set up your computer to display its menus and icons in your target language. Do the same with your iPod, iPhone or other type of mobile phone, as well as any software packages you use regularly (think Microsoft Office, iTunes, instant messenger, Skype, Internet Explorer, Mozilla Firefox, Safari and friends). If you're spending six or more hours a day in front of a computer, plenty of words will be hard-wired into your brain in no time at all.

Finding Guinea Pigs: Practice Makes (Almost) Perfect

"I don't have anyone to practise with."

Many of us have been in this situation before. It can be challenging to find conversation partners and situations where you can put your now sky-rocketed language skills to good use. I'm here to tell you that it's only temporary. There are several easy ways to find willing, able guinea pigs and other stages to practise speaking, listening, writing and interrogating.

Ask your friends for help
This one is obvious, but unless your friends know you want to practise with them, they'll likely revert to speaking in English with you. If you're lucky enough to have friends who speak the language you want to speak, don't let it go to waste. Ask them for help, and be persistent. It will pay off.

Explore Language Exchanges

There are hundreds of websites which list people looking for language exchanges. The idea is that you both want to learn and practice. There are no specific rules, but you might, for example, meet with a French-speaker who wants to practise their English. Over a coffee, meal, or sitting in a park, you speak for half an hour in English and half an hour in French.

In my experience, three of the best ways to find language exchange partners are:

1. General "advertisement" websites, such as gumtree.com and craiglist.com. These websites allow users to post any kind of advertisement from adopting pets to selling guitars, but have a section on language exchange.

2. Specific websites for language exchange.
Google "Language Exchange [Your target language]" and several websites will appear, with prospective exchangers. www.couchsurfing.com is another great option (look for people willing to meet for a coffee).

3. Universities. As an attractive place for international students, universities usually have huge diversity in students with multiple languages, and regularly offer language exchange services (either formal or informal). By asking a Japanese lecturer, I found a Japanese language exchange partner when I was studying and this helped me immensely (not to mention giving me 'creative help' with my homework).

Eat yourself into happiness

Rather than visiting your usual restaurants, try visiting an authentic international restaurant with staff who speak your target language (for example, an Italian restaurant for those who want to learn Italian). Try ordering in the language, ask questions, learn the names of the food in that language, and use it as a way to familiarise yourself with the words and culture at the same time.

Listen to music

Gone are the days of having to dig into grandma's record collection. These days it's easy to find music in other languages. Most good record stores sell CDs in a variety of languages. Spotify, iTunes and Amazon are constantly adding more international music to their selections, and I find they have an excellent range for most major languages.

To understand the lyrics, it's now easier than ever to find them using the internet. Just Google the title of the song and the name of the artist, and you're likely to find several pages with the lyrics, which you can then translate if you like. www.wordreference.com is a great translation resource. Combined with podcasts, listening to multilingual music during downtime is a fantastic way to boost your skills very quickly.

If you don't want to buy or just want a sample, use Youtube.com to search for your artist and listen to a few songs for free.

Get your kids involved (if you have them)

If your kids are language-inclined – or if you want them to be – get them started early. I don't have kids, but friends of mine who do tell me this is one excellent way to keep focused on learning, and make your kids part of the process instead of keeping them separate while you learn. Teach them a few phrases they can use in English: open the door, where's your friend, how was school today. Anything to get them started and vested in the process.

Action Plan

This is a long one. You'll get out what you put in. Ready?

1. Find one event you can attend in the next three months that involves speakers of your target language. Get others involved if you can, and go to it. Buy the ticket now if you can.

2. If you take public transport or walk in a busy area, keep an ear out for people speaking your target language. Even if you're not confident to approach them at first, try to eavesdrop and understand what they're saying. When you're ready, initiate a quick conversation in that language: ("Hi! I just heard you speaking Russian... can I ask where you're from?")

3. Encourage your classmates to speak in your target language instead of English, and put your teacher's pet hat on.

4. If you have pets, find out three phrases you can use with them in your target language. If people look at you strangely, tell them it's an experiment you're doing to help you remember more words.

5. Set up your computer, mobile phone, or MP3 player to function in your target language.

6. Find at least one good outlet to practise: a friend, language exchange or colleague.

7. Listen to two songs in the next two weeks, and look up the lyrics to digest their meaning

Why Being Given A False Identity Can Be A Compliment

The Oompah band played loudly in the background, the smell of delicious wheat beer permeated the cool winter air, and every now and then a fellow in Lederhosen (German leather pants) would wander past with another litre of beer in hand, leaving me more astounded at his drinking abilities every time he passed.

Potatoes and sauerkraut filled the tables in front of me, laughter roared almost everywhere, and I thought things couldn't possibly get any better in this small beer hall in Munich. Then things did get even better.

"Are you Swiss?" asked a local two seats down from me.

This was, at the time, the biggest compliment anyone had ever paid my German (even if it was a slightly strangely worded compliment). I beamed from ear to ear. He genuinely wanted to know whether I was Swiss.

Why?

I was speaking in German to my friend at the table. The Swiss have a distinctly unique form of spoken German - Swiss German - which is different to the high German spoken throughout most of Germany.

My neighbour had picked up the fact that I wasn't a native High German speaker, but thought it close enough that maybe I was a native speaker of a different dialect. In effect, he had said "*Your German sounds sort of, almost, close to being something resembling a native. Could it be that you're from an area that speaks a little differently than we do, and your strange accent stands out in this beer hall?*".

As I said, a strangely worded compliment. For me, it was one of the best achievements I've had with my German. Why? Because rather than asking me in English - which would have been a telltale sign that he knew I wasn't a native German speaker at all - he had asked 'why does your German sound a bit weird?'.

I'm still not Swiss, and that will never change. Little did he know, it was my English-speaking accent shining through in my German which gave me away as a possible Swissie, but I was happy to have come that far. Maybe one day someone will ask if I am Austrian.

Elated, I promptly grinned and replied that I wasn't Swiss, but Australian, and proceeded to have a very nice conversation with this rather drunk friendly fellow.

When you're asked questions like this, learn to recognise when someone is pointing out how far you've come with your language. It may not be perfect (like my experience with pretending to be Swiss), but it's a significant achievement and one you should use as motivation to keep you going.

PART IV. Putting It All Together

The Point Of No Return: When Can You Say You're Conversationally Fluent?

BOGOTA, COLOMBIA, AUGUST 2009

I can be a stubborn man. My sister-in-law was in English mode. I was in Spanish mode. Who would win out? Her friend decided for me.

'He keeps responding to you in Spanish. Why do you keep answering him in English? Stop being so rude!' he joked.

It's not that I didn't understand what she was saying in English. I did. But we were in Colombia, I only had a month there, and I wasn't going to waste a night of potential practice. So I persisted, question-after-question, responding in Spanish even when she spoke to me in English.

I told you I was stubborn. Why did I do this?

I was testing a theory: that I had passed the point of no return. I believe this is the point when it becomes just as easy for a bilingual native speaker to respond to you in your target language as it is for them to respond to you in English.

For example: when I first started learning Spanish, the conversation above would have been very difficult for me. It would have been easier for both my sister-in-law and I to have the conversation in English.

As my Spanish improved, I reached a point where it was about the same level of difficulty to speak in English as in Spanish. Now (on a good day), I can speak to my Colombian relatives just as well in Spanish as I could if we spoke in English about most topics.

The wonderful effects of this are two-fold:
1. Your conversations become more natural because there's no need to switch between languages ('code switch') anymore
2. You get more practice, because if you're in a group, you can fit right in and not have to translate from one language to another.

I personally believe that, once you have reached this point, you can say that you are conversationally fluent in that language.

Well, am I fluent or not?

Depending on who you talk to, there are many different definitions of being fluent. Some common examples, from strictest definition to more lenient:

- You can read and write academic texts at the same level in both languages
- You can recognise and recall lists of complex words equally quickly in both languages
- You can get by speaking this language in daily life
- You can speak with someone equally as well in their language as you could in your own. It's not painful for your Spanish-speaking friend to speak to you in Spanish.

Like all subjective assessments, these definitions are all, in some way, flawed. The only thing that's important is that you make your own definition. The last one is my definition, and when I believe you can also say you are fluent.

"I can have a smooth conversation at normal speed about most topics with a speaker of [your target language], and it's not painful for them. It's about the same level of ease as if we were speaking in English."

Now you're rocking: do a good deed

After you've become conversationally fluent, I believe it's helpful for both you and others to do some good deeds. Help beginners with their grammar. Pass your passion for the language on to other people, and encourage them in their own learning journey. Share interesting things about the language with them. Teach, show, and share. If it weren't for people along the way who encouraged me, taught me and inspired me, my journey would have been much more difficult.

That is why I wrote this guide – to share all I've learned along the way.

Teaching others also reinforces the concepts you've learned. When I started teaching beginner Spanish, I had to reflect back to the books I studied at the first level to make sure I was teaching the correct rules to students. Because I'd learned them some time ago, I'd forgotten some of how the rules were formed.

Revising this, along with the higher levels as I taught more, really helped solidify my baseline Spanish. It also helped me to teach my students the right way.

An example of how this can really be done

Meet Sarah. Sarah has two Argentinean friends and visited an Argentinean restaurant last week, where they talked about the delicious food, danced a little tango and she heard her friends ordering in their smooth Argentinean accents. She was inspired, and decided to try her hand at learning Spanish.

PART I: THE BEAUTY OF BEGINNING

1. Research. Sarah searches online for "Learn Spanish Schools" and compares the top three Spanish schools in her city, looking closely at what information is given up front, course prices, locations, class times, and most importantly, the curriculum.

She finds one school with good prices ($350 for 8 weeks of 2 hours each), textbooks included, a location near her, and clearly segmented levels of achievement at each of the seven levels available. The school also offers exchange programs with universities in Spanish-speaking sister cities in Latin America and Spain, in case she wants to pursue her learning further.

She Googles the name of the school, and looks at three review websites to see what others have said about it.

The reviews look good, and she settles on this school.

2. A pact. Sarah recruits a friend to join the classes with her, and they enrol together, receiving a 10% discount of $35 each. [For more information on getting discounts at language schools, see the bonus materials at the end of this guide.]

They don't have time on the weekends for an intensive class, so opt for a two-hour class each week on Tuesday nights. They make a pact to complete at least the first two levels together.

3. Starting out. Classes begin, and Sarah takes note of only the most useful vocab and grammar, being careful not to get caught up on side notes that won't help her any time soon. Instead, she focuses on ways to interrogate her teacher in Spanish such as "Como se dice [X] en español? "How do I say [X] in Spanish?". Just using this, she finds she is at least one class ahead of her classmates.

4. Inspiration. She asks one of her friends for a recommendation on Argentinean music. Her friend suggests Diego Torres, and sends her a link to a Youtube video clip of one of his songs, complete with lyrics. She listens to the song plus two others, and enjoys the music. Next, she downloads iTunes for free and purchases one of his albums for $14.99, which comes with album artwork, and Googles the lyrics for the entire album, finding them on one single page and printing them out two-songs per page.

For now, Sarah only understands about 15% of the words in the songs, but each class she learns something new and notices her vocabulary starting to increase.

Sarah's friend doesn't know any native speakers, so Googles "Spanish Language Exchange" and finds several advertisements on Gumtree.com from native speakers in her country looking to improve their English skills. In exchange for half an hour of English over coffee, they'll happily exchange some Spanish conversation tips (free).

5. Practice. Sarah decides to schedule a dinner once a month with her Argentine friends, and asks them for some colloquial Spanish phrases during dinner. Next class, she surprises her teacher with one of the phrases and the other students sit there dumbfounded, mouths gaping at her progress.

PART II: MIND BENDING
6. More practice, and memorisation techniques. Sarah is now in the second level of her classes. She's comfortable using the basics (hello, how are you, good evening, how do I say [X], etc.), and is using them every week with her Spanish-speaking friends. Sarah's friend is doing the same with her weekly Peruvian conversation coffee partner.

Both turn their attention to making like-sounding associations with important vocab they hear during classes, with their friends, or in the Diego Torres songs. Sarah makes a concerted effort to greet her friends in Spanish, ask them how they are, and say goodbye always in Spanish.

7. Using opposites. In "Spanglish" conversations when she comes across a word she doesn't know, she asks wherever possible for the opposites of words she does know.

8. Making use of downtime. Sarah opens iTunes and searches for "Spanish Podcasts". She reads the description next to each of the seven options which appear, and focuses on those that aren't targeted at 'beginner only' or 'romantic' Spanish. (These tend to be full of cliché phrases that will get you slapped or laughed at rather than make new friends.) She finds one in particular which sounds interesting, and downloads six of their free podcasts of twelve minutes each, and transfers them to her Phone.

9. Surprising native speakers. Over the next week, Sarah spends twelve minutes of downtime on the train to and from work, listening to one of the podcasts each way. She learns four new phrases and surprises her Argentine friends at their next dinner, and her teacher before the next class, by using one of them in context.

10. More practice. Again. She starts to see many of the links between Spanish and English, and starts guessing from the context. [If your language doesn't have a close relationship with English, don't worry: this is just a minor step and is not critical]. She finds that her Argentine friends still usually understand what she's saying even if the word she guessed at doesn't exist, and they usually correct her.

PART III: TO BECOME FLUENT, SPEAK YOU MUST
11. Making the language part of daily life. Both girls continue on into the third, fourth and fifth levels of the Spanish courses, and take a one-hour joint extra tutoring class to practise together ($35 per hour split between the two of them = $17.50 each per week).

In the meantime, they continue to download more music, podcasts, watch videos on YouTube, rent Spanish movies once per month, attend film and food festivals, and speak with their friends. They're now able to have a great conversation in Spanish. Even though they still make some mistakes, they can get their point across with minimal effort and speak Spanish 80% of the time in class and to their tutor.

12. Travel, and crossing the point of no return. Sarah decides to enrol in an exchange program through the Spanish school. When she arrives, her host family is already surprised at how advanced her Spanish is. Her host family's brother spent time in the US and so speaks very good English.

She persists in answering him in Spanish, and after two days he gives up trying to reply to her in English and addresses her completely in Spanish [success!]. She offers to speak with him in English every day over breakfast so he can practise.

(Notice how this now looks like a favour, and both are winners. Sarah wants to take advantage of the native-speaking environment, and has just passed the point of no return. Her host brother is also able to practise his English, but in a confined timeframe. Win-win.)

13. Recognising progress & doing good deeds. When Sarah returns from Peru, she contacts her friend who has also made good progress. They both feel comfortable speaking, reading and writing Spanish, and offer to help another friend who had taken the first level and dropped out.

Now it's your turn

Now we've seen all of the techniques I've learned to take language learning from complete beginner to conversationally fluent, as well as a real example of how this can be done. This is just the beginning. Now it's your turn: try out what's feasible for you (I hope all or most will be useful), practice making language learning a part of your everyday lifestyle, and it is my sincere hope that you'll soon be dominating your foreign language.

I wish you all the best and thanks again for picking up this guide. I really appreciate your support.

And remember: language learning doesn't have to be a difficult process. If you make it part of your daily lifestyle, you'll be speaking like a local in no time. Enjoy and happy speaking,

Tristan King

Bonus Information and Closing

Bonus: Tips For Getting Discounts On Language Courses

There are five ways I've found to get discounts on language courses. Here they are:

1. Recruit a friend, pay together.
Many people study together, but pay individually. If you pay together instead, you can often get a discount. My wife and I studied French together, in the same class. By paying in one instalment, we saved 15%. This can add up to a significant amount if you take several courses, and even just as a once-off, it's worth coordinating.

2. Student discounts.
If you're a student, ask whether there are student or concession discounts. There often are. You might need to quote your student number (although I've found this is often not checked rigorously, meaning you could theoretically give any number. Be careful, though.)

3. Early bird specials.
It's in language schools' best interest to know numbers in advance. To do this, they often promote an 'early bird special' of 5-10% if you book by a certain date. When you're looking around, keep an eye out for such specials, and utilise them if you can book and pay in advance.

4. Last minute specials.
Language schools also like to fill up their classes. After all, they have to pay the teacher the same rate whether there are five or fifteen students in a class. If you missed the early bird special, ask whether there are any 'last minute discounts'. Several schools I know will offer this to encourage fence-sitters to join the class at the last minute. Think of it like getting discounted tickets on a plane at the eleventh hour.

5. Book more than one course at a time.
If you're committed to studying more than one level, ask whether discounts are available for bulk bookings. Some schools will encourage students to enrol in, for example, the first two levels at a 10% discount. This gets them more bookings, and also drives a deeper commitment in students: because they have already paid for the course, they're more likely to attend.

You made it to the end!

Thanks for joining me here.

Thank you so much for picking up *Conquering Foreign Languages*.. I really hope you enjoyed it, and that it helped you come up with creative ideas to learn and continue learning languages.

If you'd like to give feedback on the book, or to find more self-development books for learning, join me at BigActionBooks.com.

Thanks again,
Tristan and The Big Action Books team

 BIG ACTION BOOKS

BigActionBooks.com

Footnotes

[1] According to Wikipedia in June 2011 (when this book was originally written), there are 390 million Spanish speakers, 123 million Japanese speakers, and 118 million German speakers in the world. Will I ever speak with all 631 million of these people? Of course not. But think of the possibilities. For more on this, and other good reasons to learn a language, see this book's companion site at languagemusings.com.

[2] I don't have any fancy three-letter combinations after my name, and this is one reason why my advice is practical and not solely academic. In the meantime, if you'd like to see my qualifications, you can find me on LinkedIn.

[3] If you don't know what a 'verb table' is yet, consider yourself lucky. As Massive Attack rightly noted in their song "Teardrop", a verb is a doing word. Conjugating a verb means changing it depending on who is doing the doing: 'I play', 'he plays'. Most language classes involve sorting verbs and their relevant conjugations into tables to memorise. In this section, I include a few tips to get over the wall and move on to the fun stuff.

[4] A note about Intellectual Property here, because I don't want to get in trouble with Rambo. Rambo is Copyrighted and was produced by the production company Anabasis N.V in 1982. Further details can be found at http://www.imdb.com/title/tt0083944/.

[5] Not her real name

[6] Note: I have zero financial interest in Apple and their devices. I'm only recommending them because I use them myself and have found them to work very well.

Acknowledgements

I'm indebted to many people for giving me the inspiration to write this guide, and to many others for the extra help they gave me along the way.

Thanks to JP Villanueva for your constant encouragement, help with proofreading, and for being an all-round language guru.

To Matt for keeping me going, making suggestions on content and layout, and for telling me that the advice was worth sharing.

To Brendan for proofreading the manuscript, giving lots of great ideas and being a big fan of the fictional monkey character introduced earlier.

To my parents for always encouraging me to do what I was passionate about, and to my friend Silvia, for being the inspiration to learn Spanish, which resulted in the development of many of the techniques explained in this guide.

About the author

Tristan King is a serial language fanatic: teacher, student and writer. He speaks (at the time of writing) Japanese, Spanish, German, Italian, French, and is learning Indonesian.

Notes

Notes

_____

_____

_____

_____

_____

_____

_____

_____

_____

_____

Notes

Notes

Notes

Notes

Notes

Notes

Notes

Notes

Notes

Notes

Notes

Notes

Conquering Foreign Languages

Big Action Books

Notes

Notes

Notes

Notes

_____

_____

_____

_____

_____

_____

_____

_____

_____

_____

Notes

Notes

Notes

Made in the USA
Las Vegas, NV
02 November 2023

80133724R00044